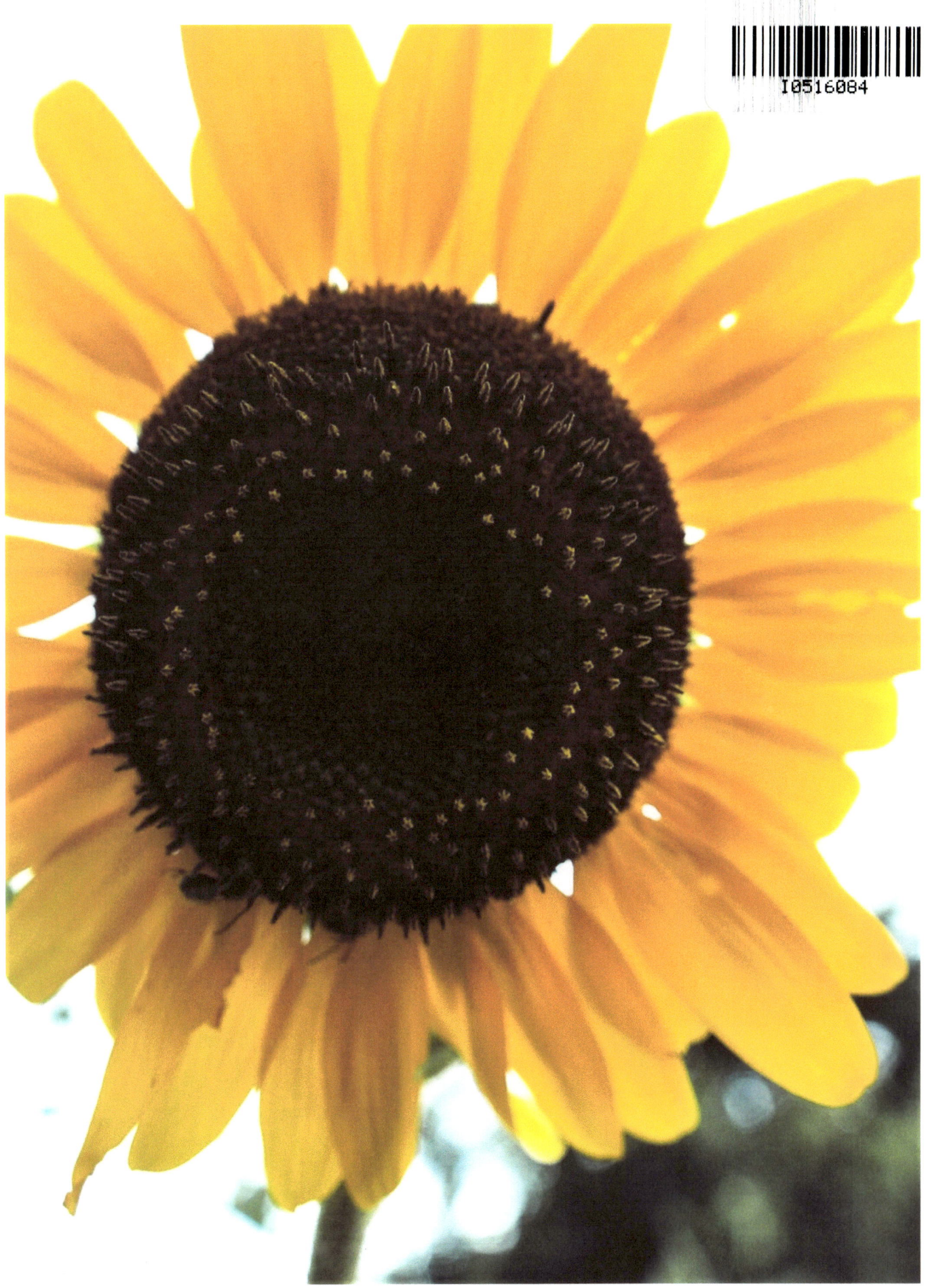

Flower Love
Pictures and Petite Poems

By

Gabrielle Angel Lilly

Book 1 of the Pictures and Poems by Angel Lilly Series

Flower Love

Pictures and Petite Poems

By Gabrielle Angel Lilly

Pictures and Poems by Angel Lilly, Book 1

Photographs by Gabrielle Angel Lilly, 2019

Published by FunFast, GAL Media, 1000 Words Press

ISBN: 978-1-7326698-0-2

January 2020

All Rights Reserved.

*Dedicated to everyone who loves love,
or who would like to learn to love love,
or who is learning to love loving.*

Many thanks to all things bright and beautiful, all things dark and sweet, all things known and unknown, knowing and unknowing... Thank you.

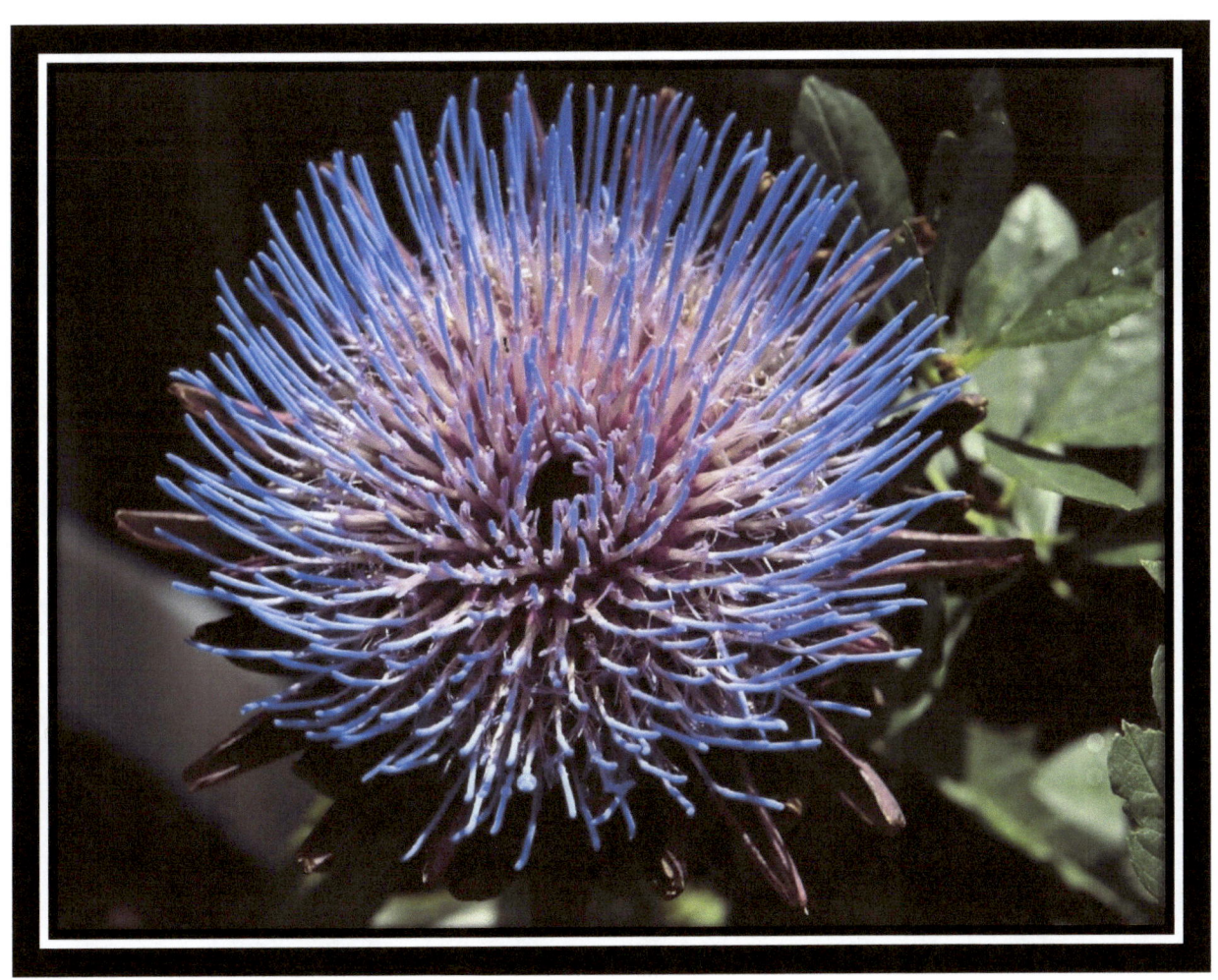

You shine with unlimited mystery and great potential.
I love the way you brush by me.

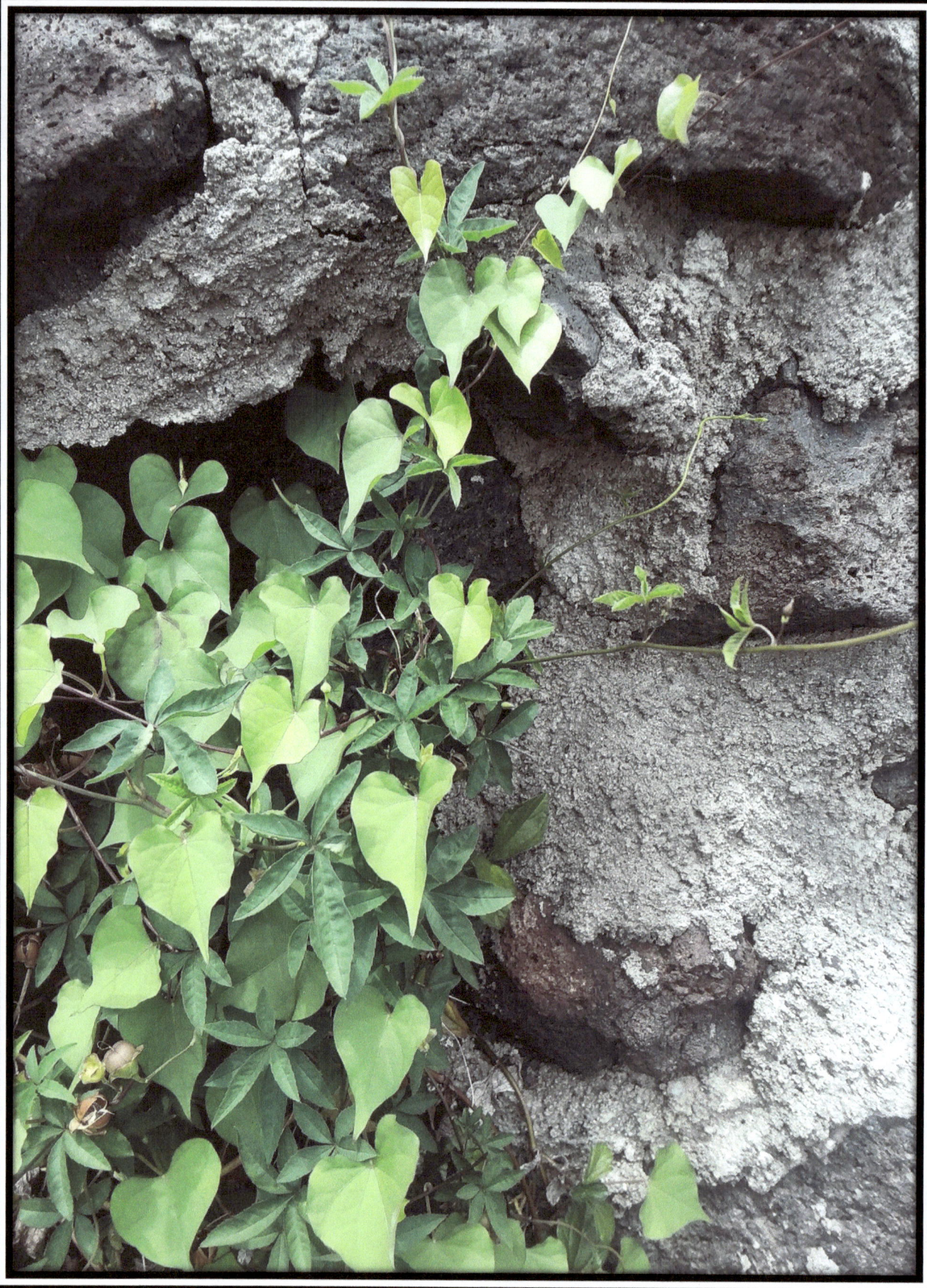

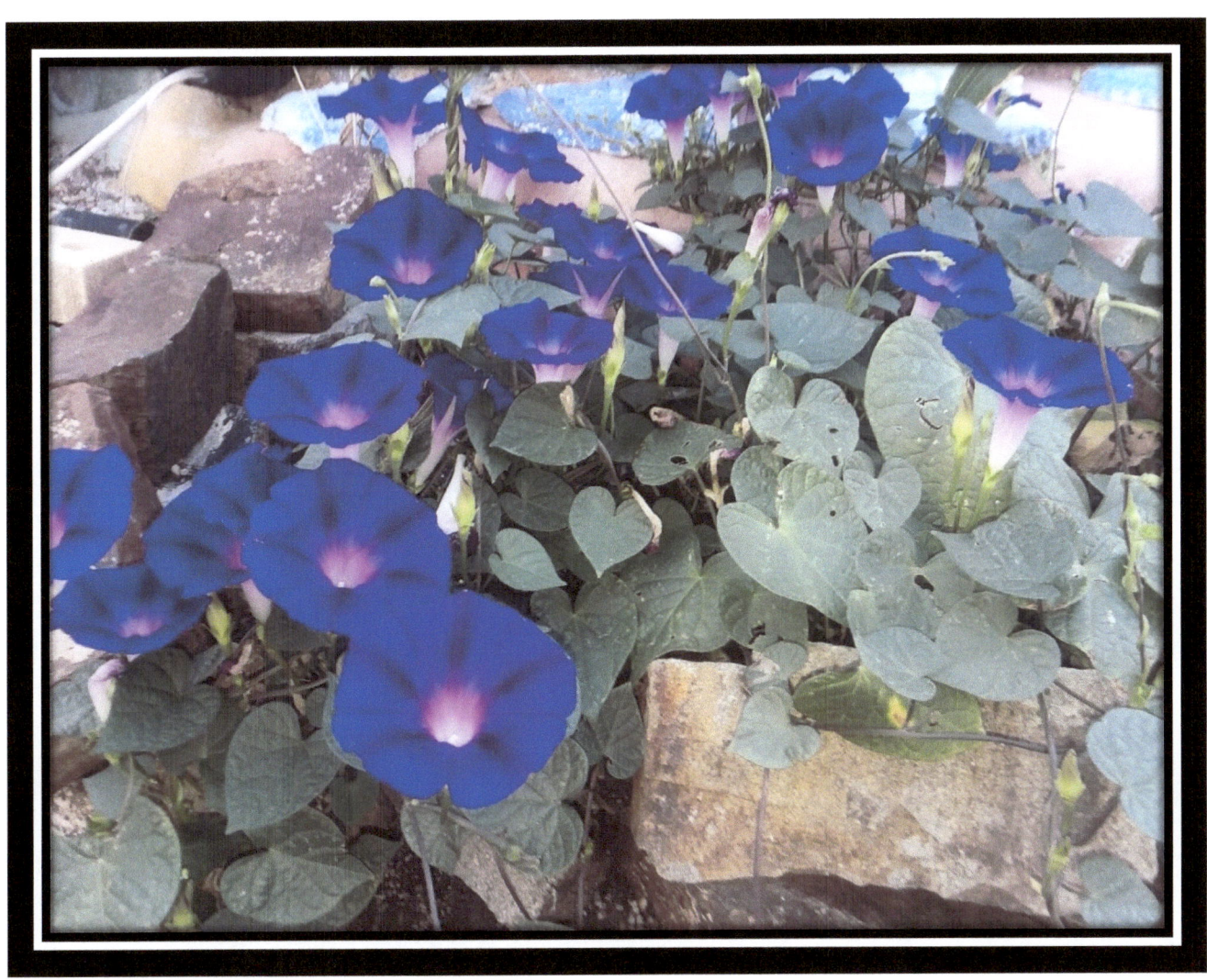

Under everything is our hearts, beating.

Your colors are magnetic to me.

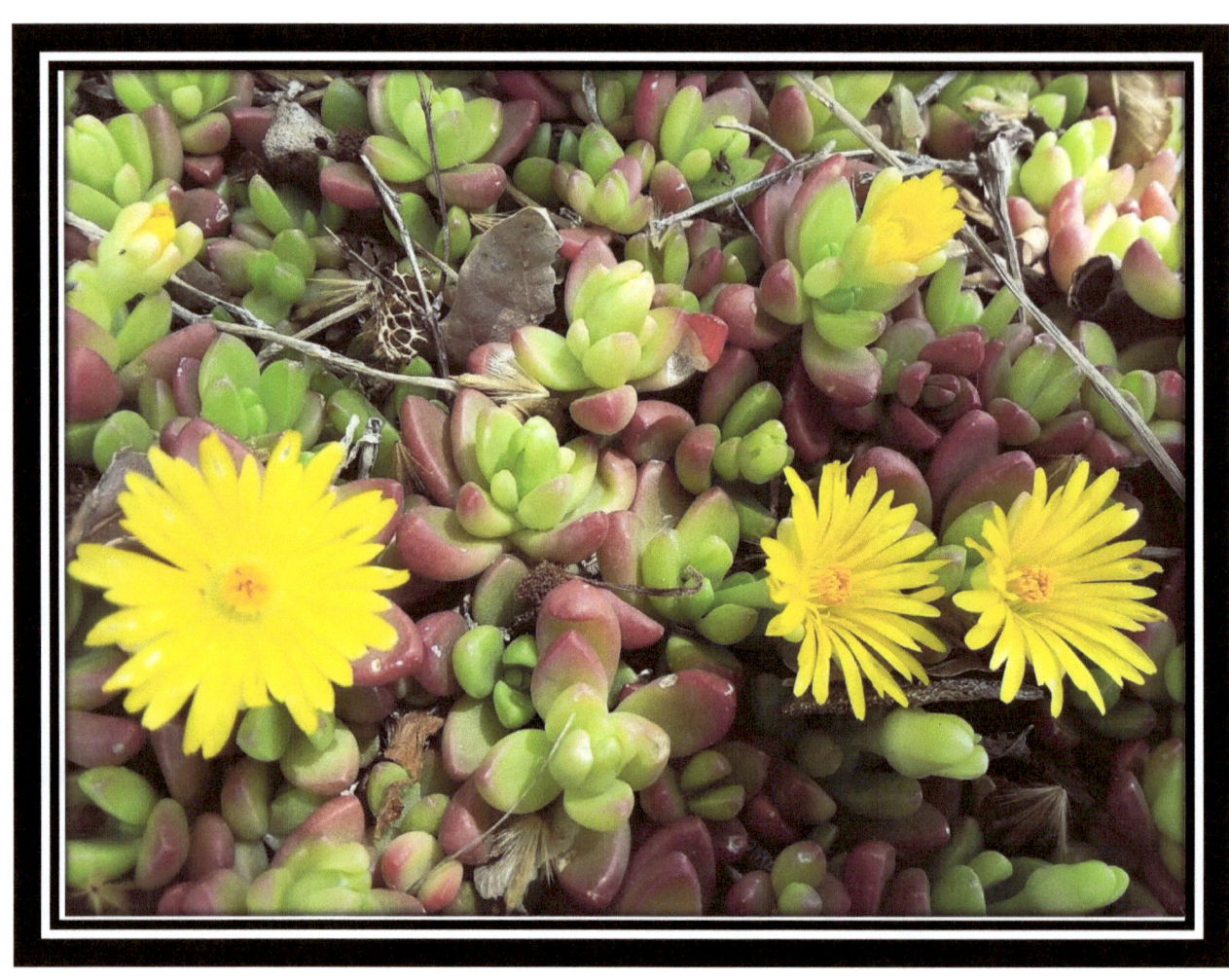

You are The One. I am The One.
We have always been the ones.

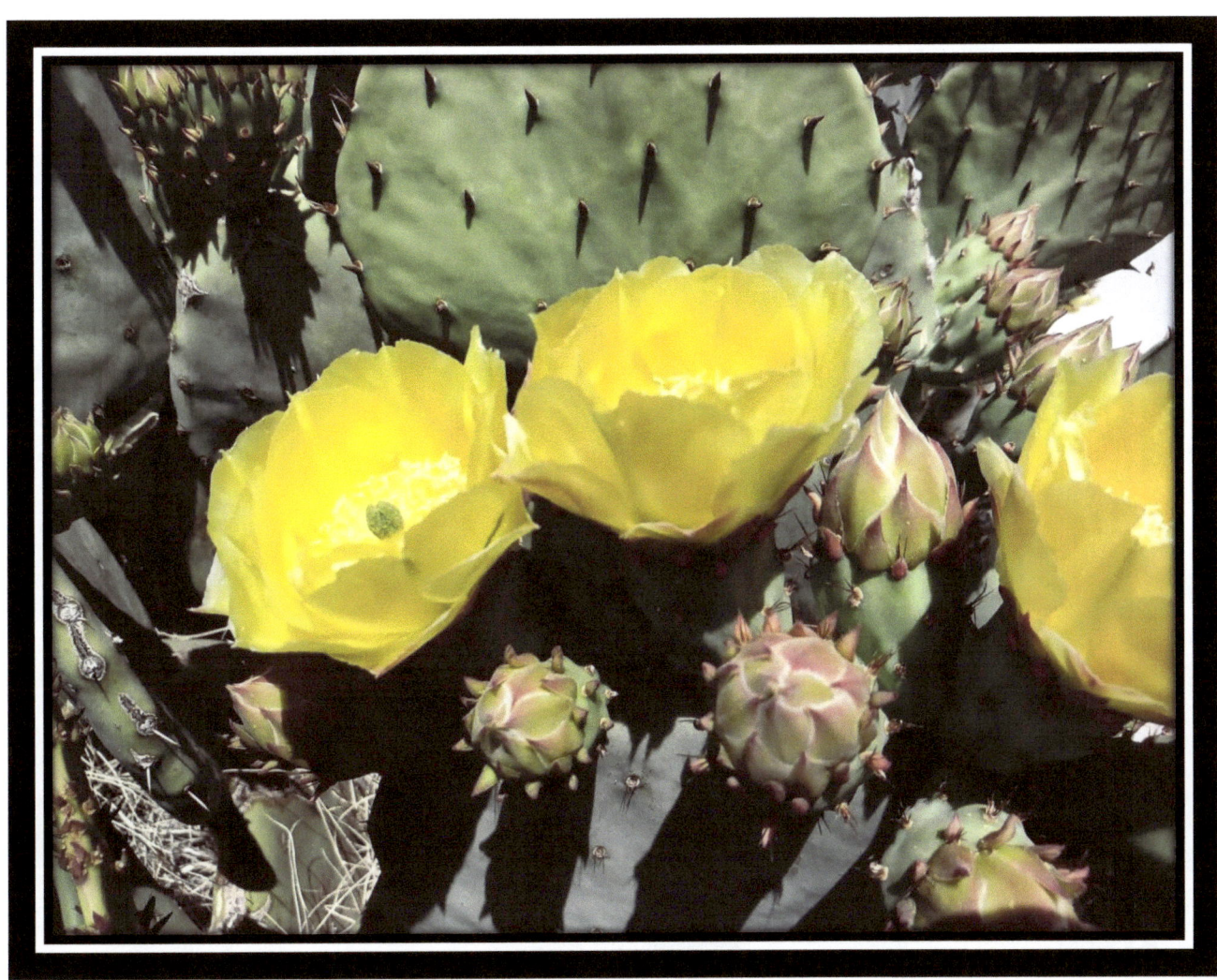

Oh! How I love to watch you bloom.
Unfolding as you do; so perfect.

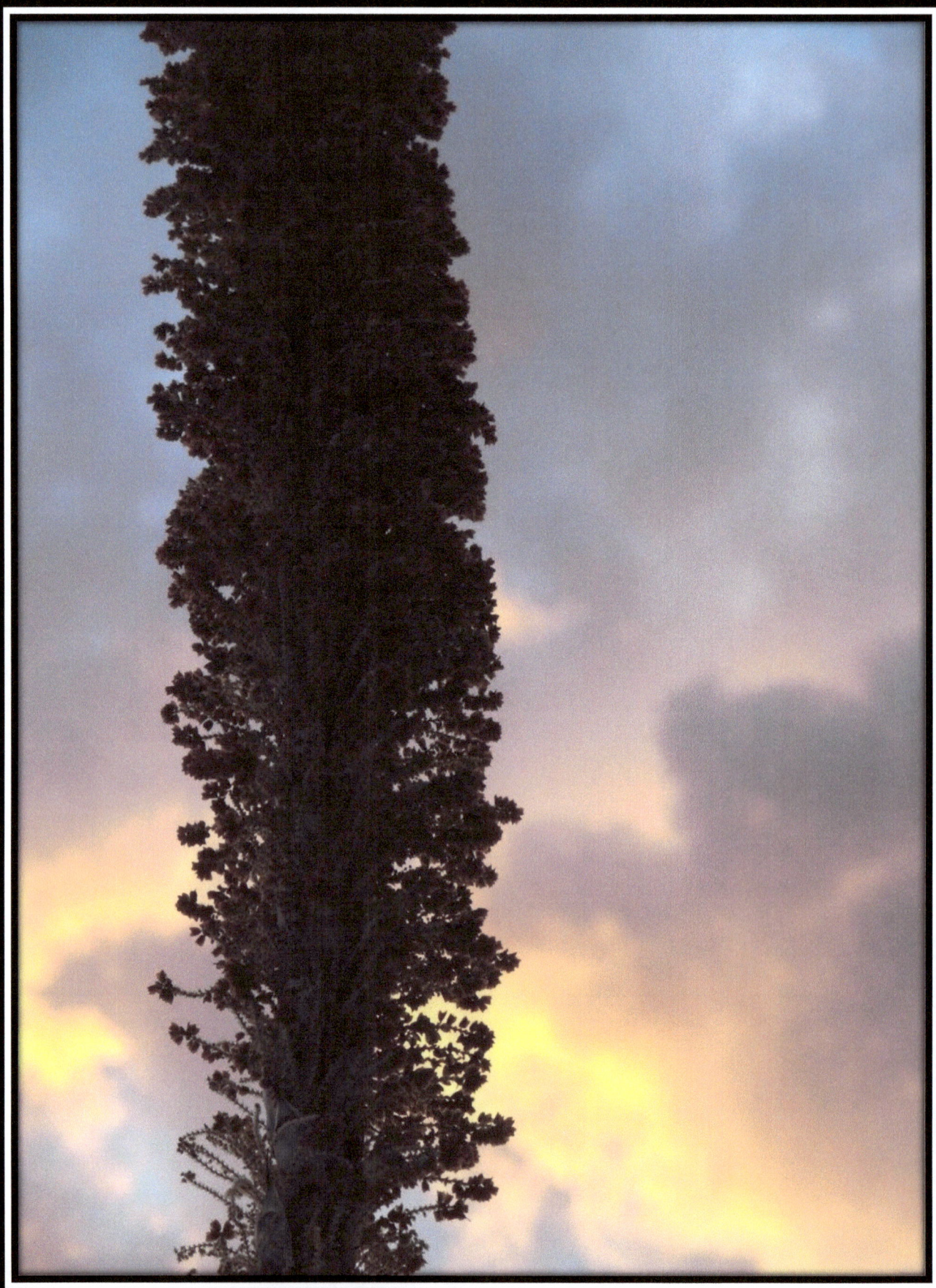

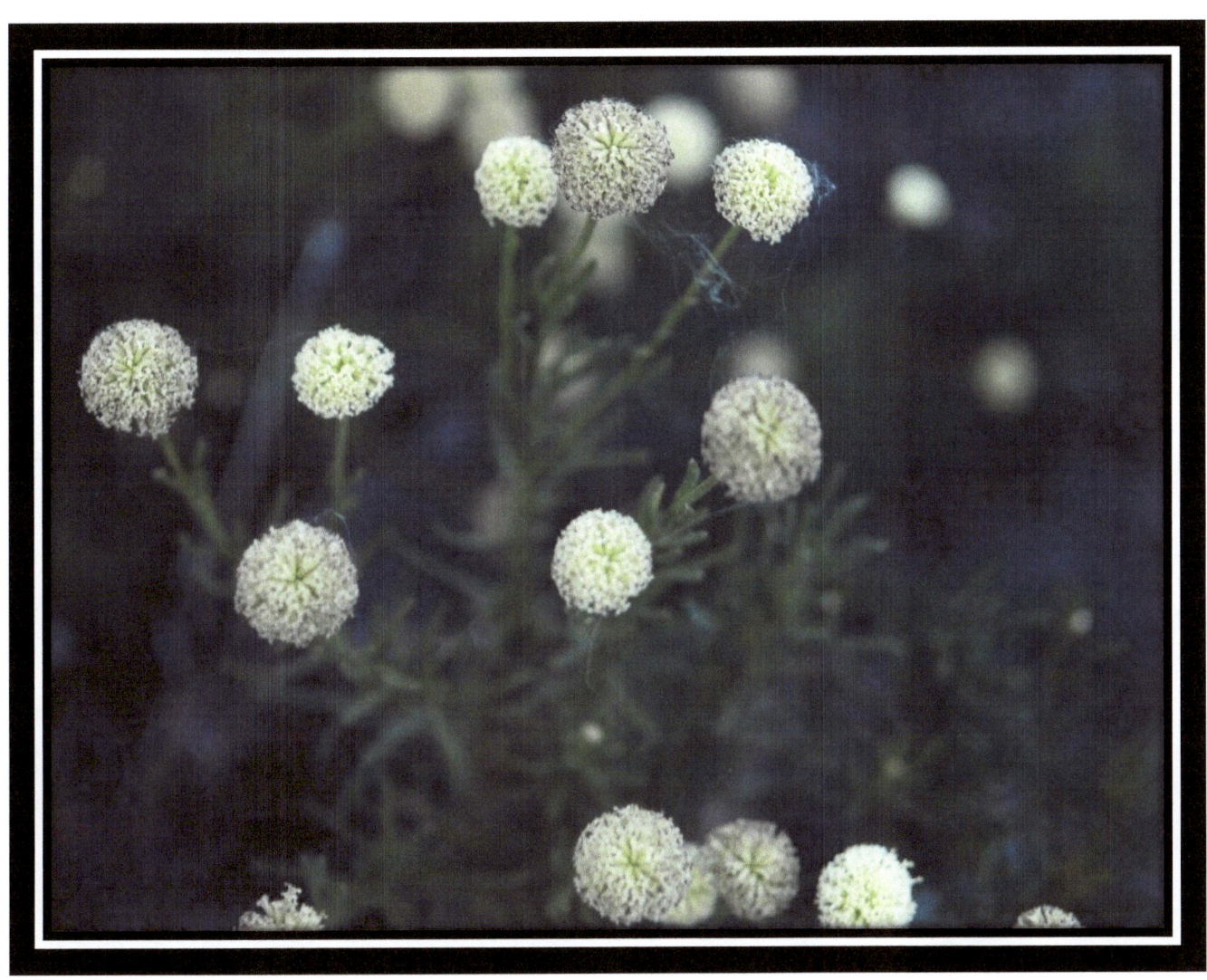

Now is your time, baby!
You got this.
Shine.

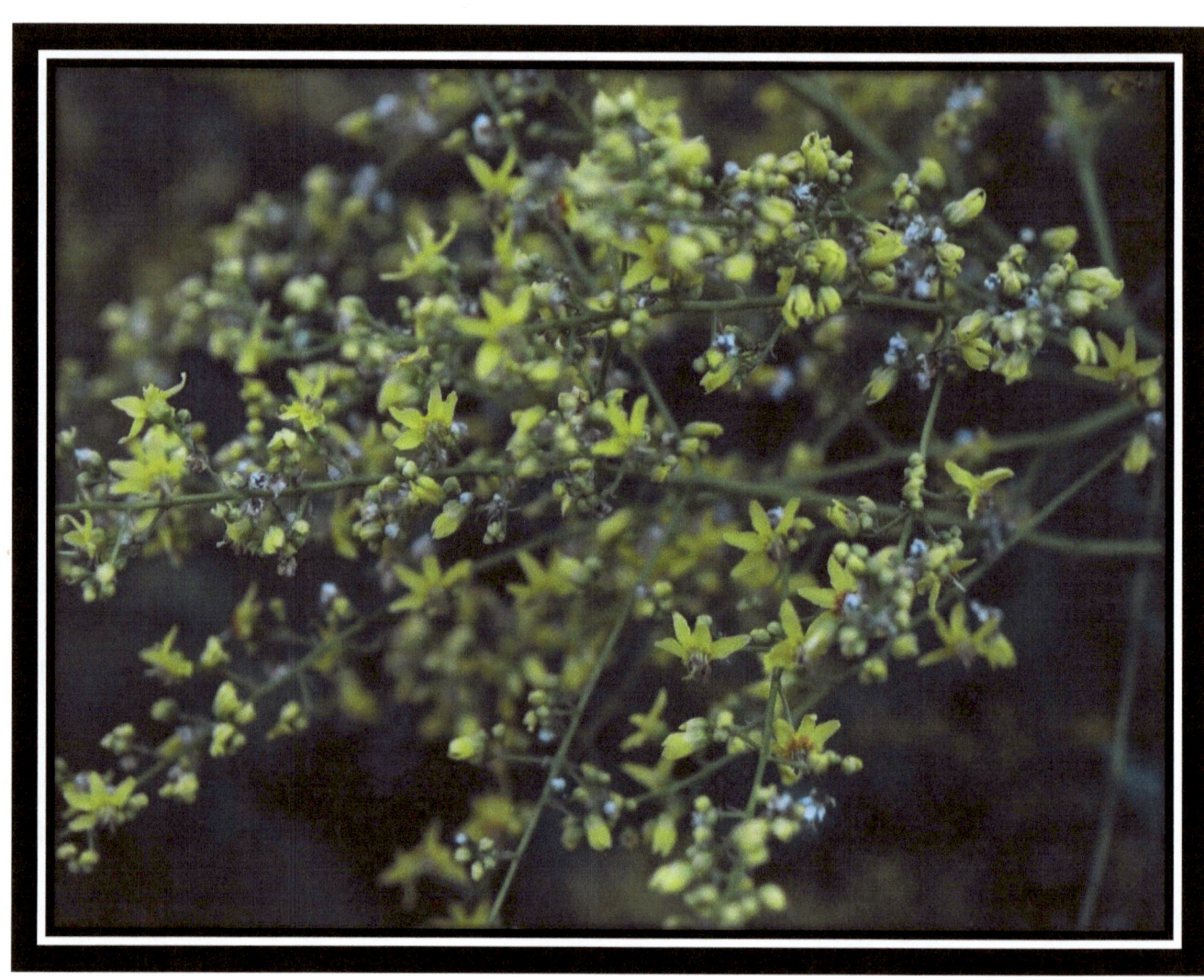

So many of the tiniest
and largest things are perfect about you.
I lose count of them all.
You are always exactly what you need to be
in every moment.

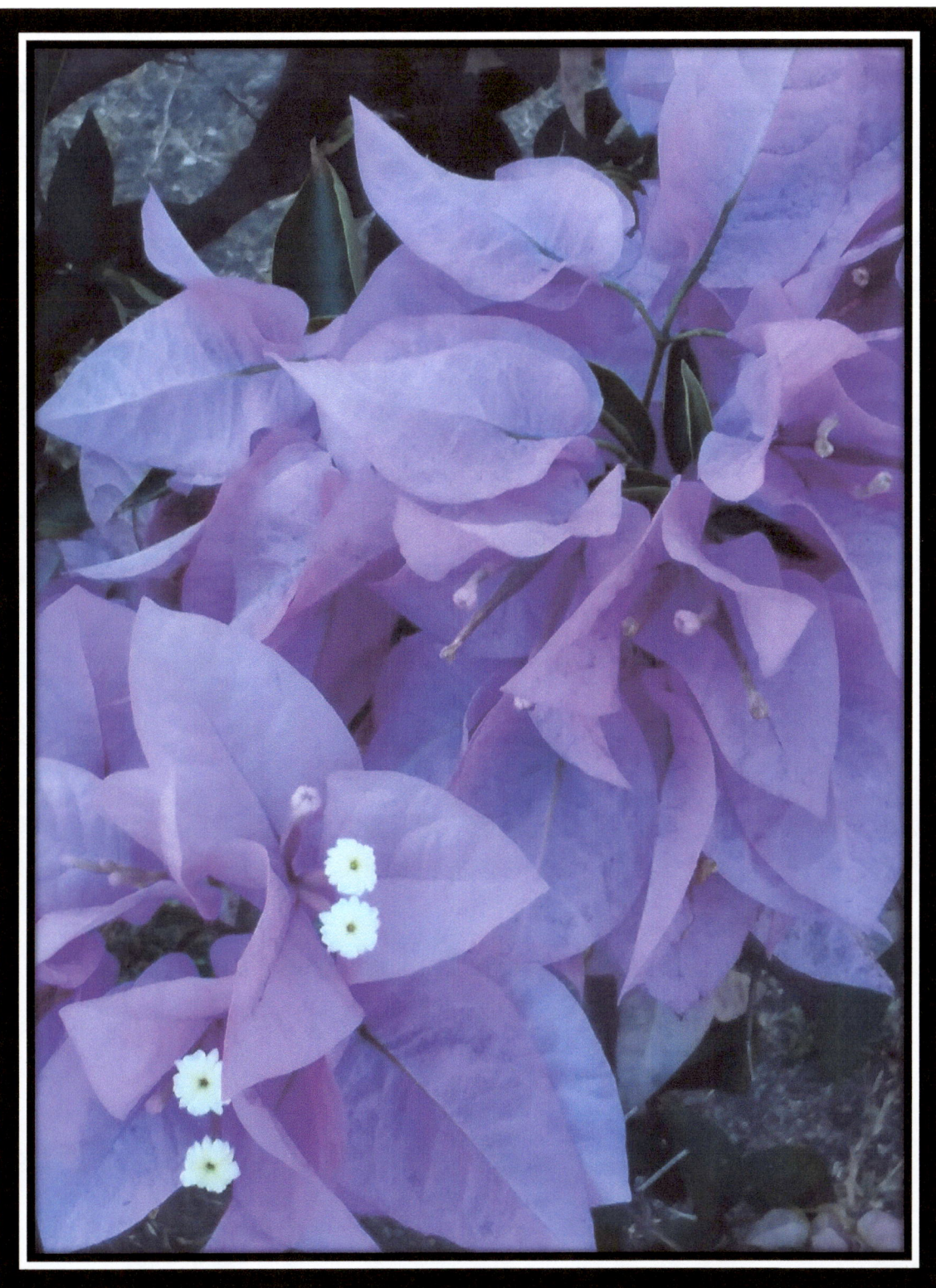

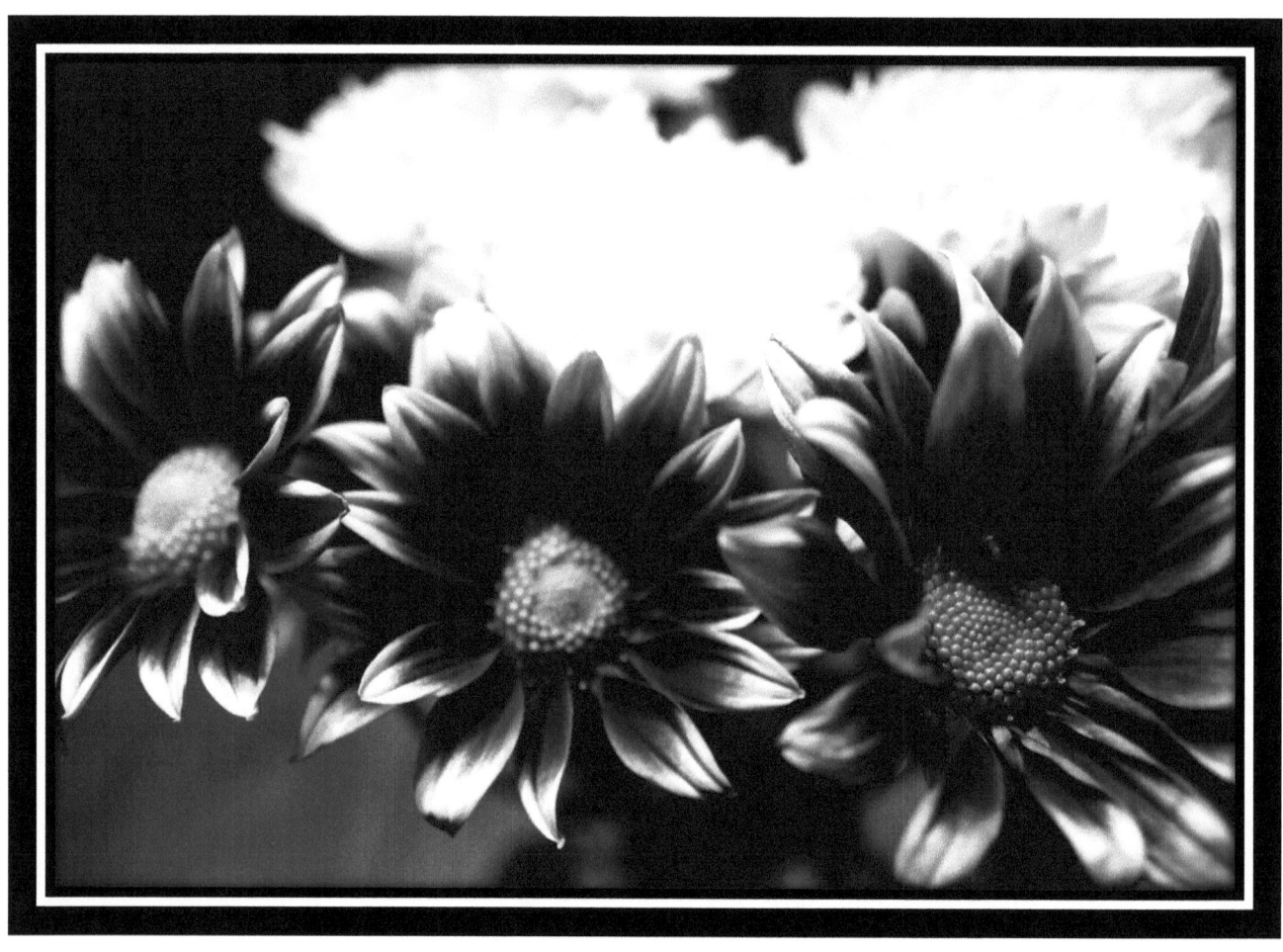

At the beginning and end of every day
it comes down to one binary choice.
Choose love. Choose lighter. Choose a little bit better.

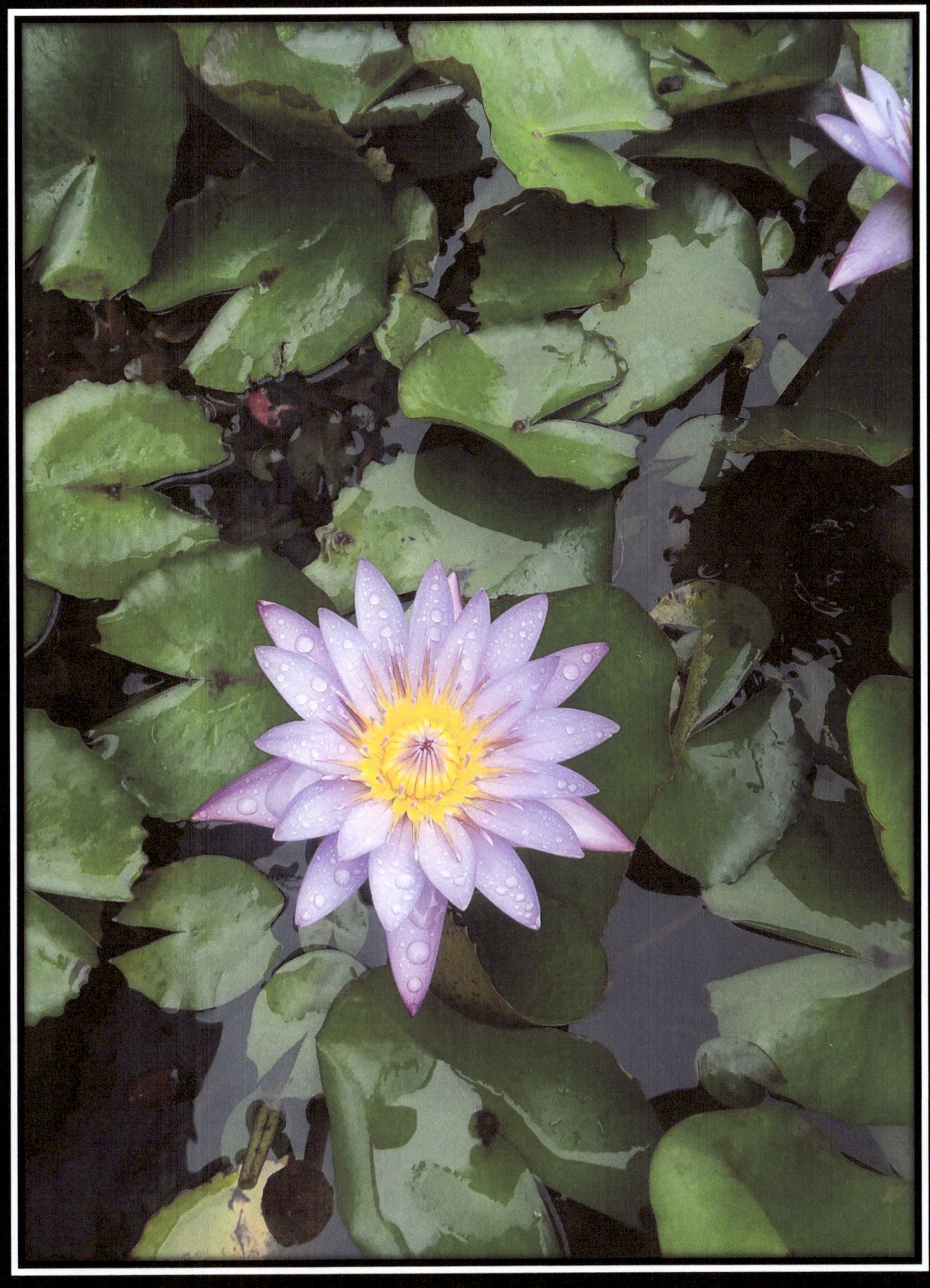

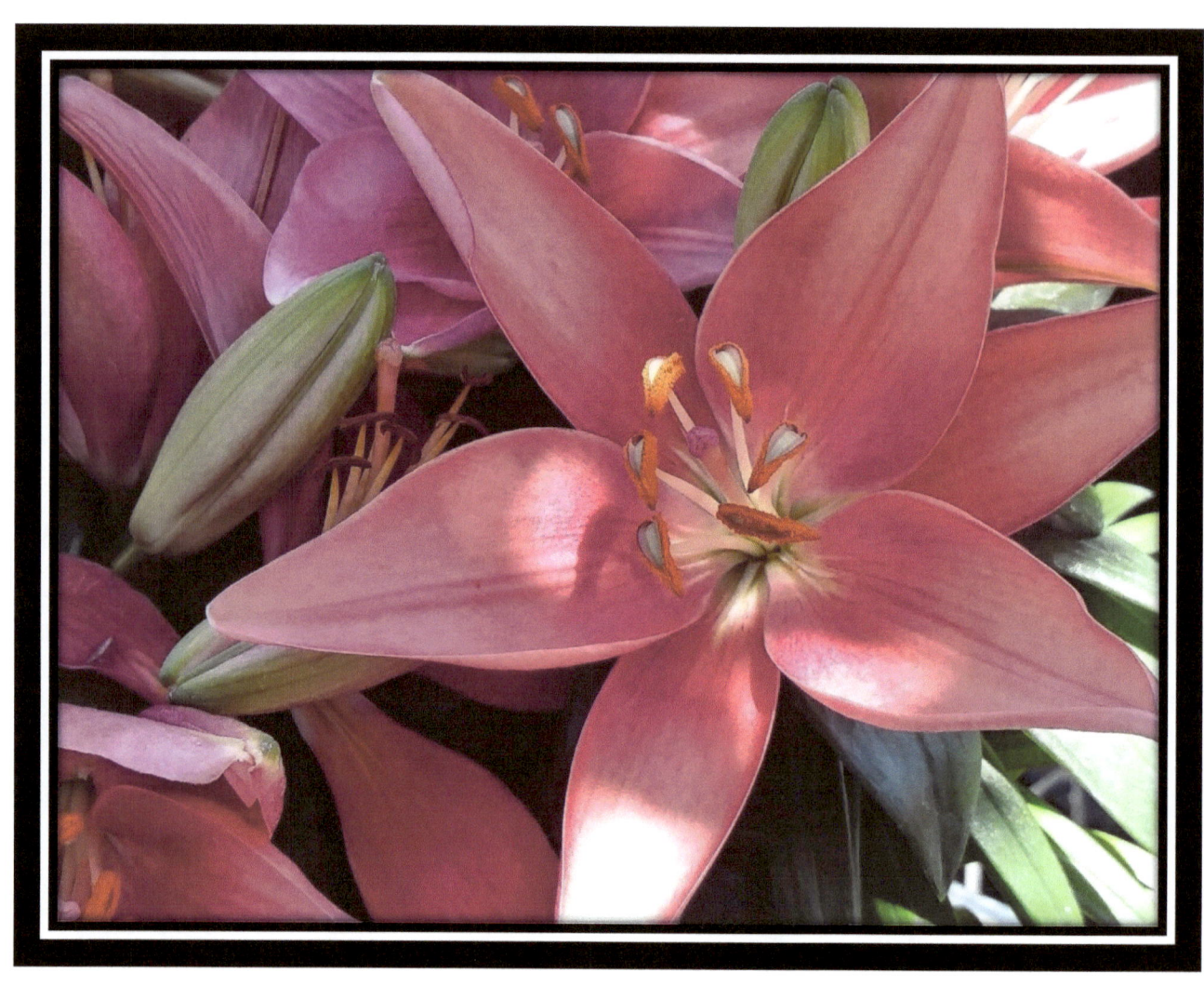

Rhaar, baby!

The super fantastic vibrant perfectly timed and placed

arrangement that is you

certainly is superb!

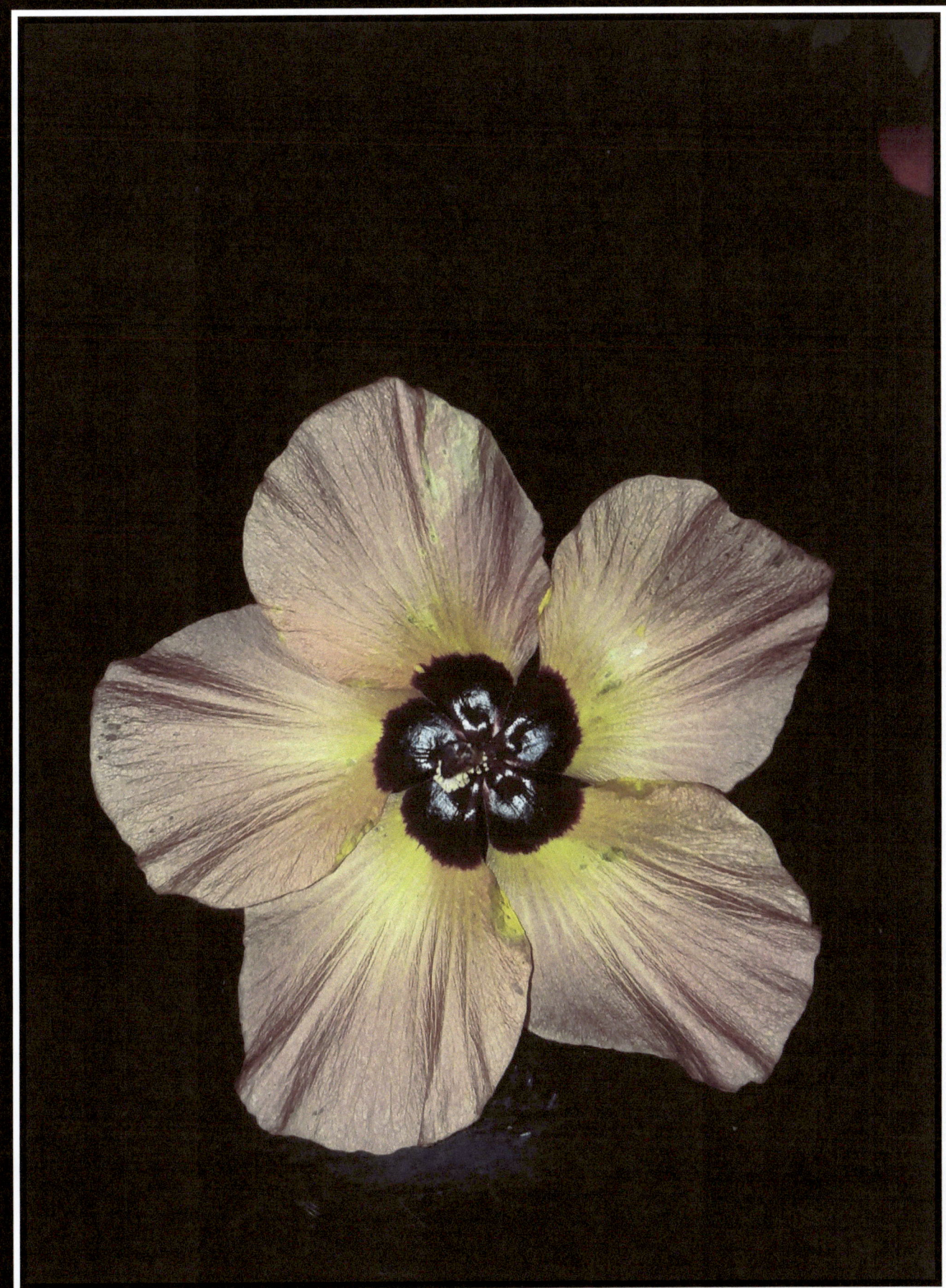

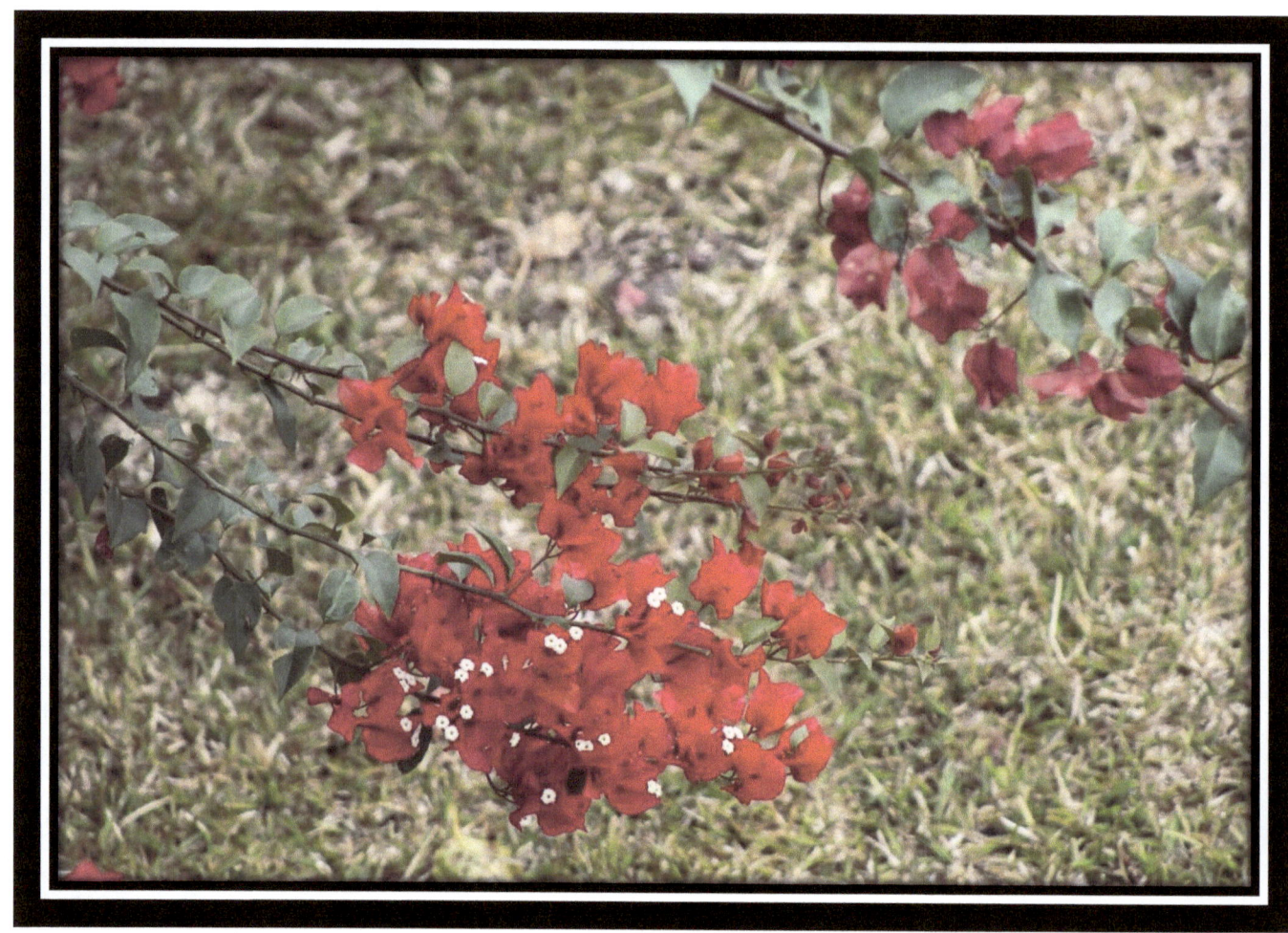

*Sometimes we don't have much to say
and that is perfect.*

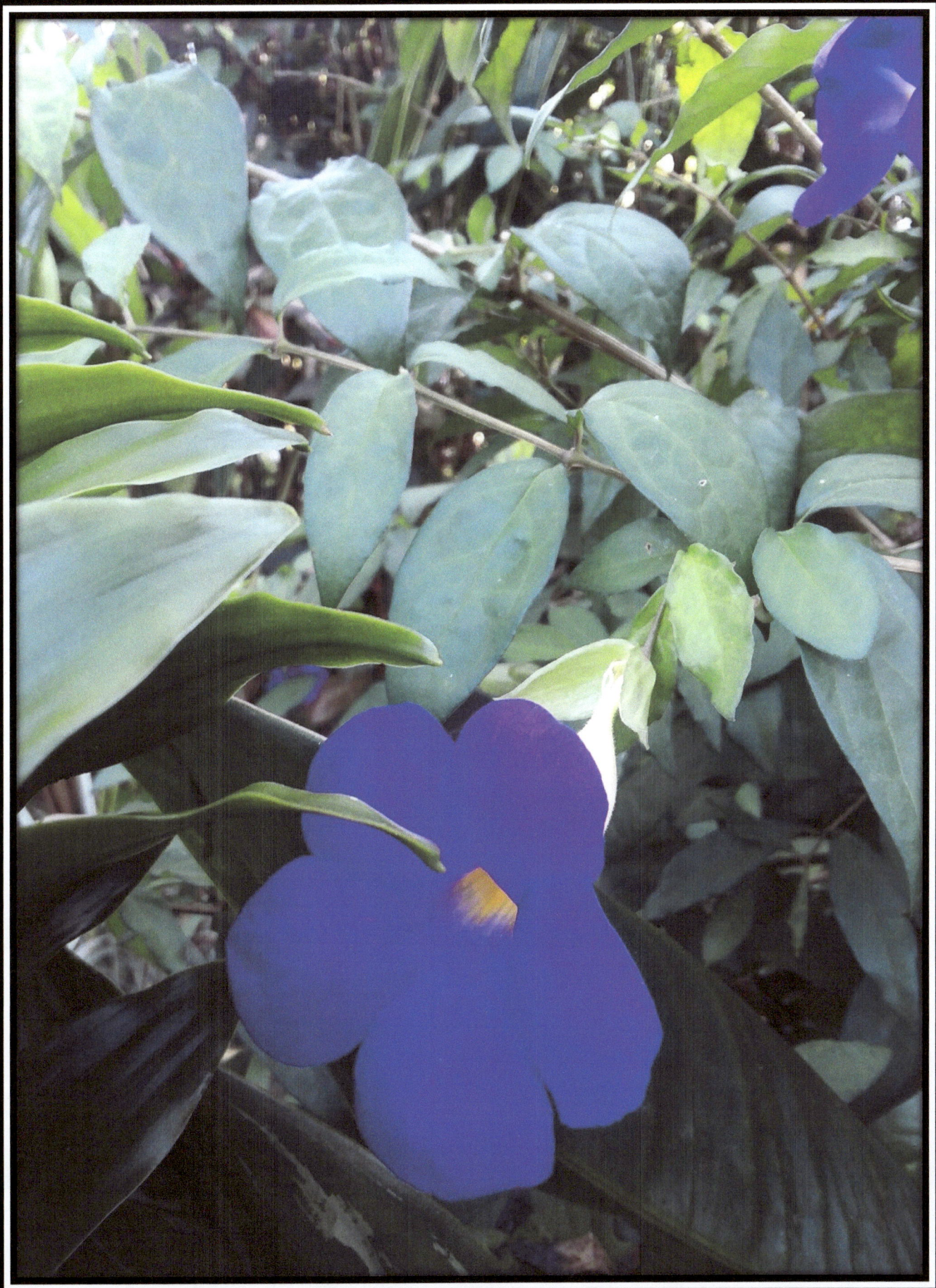

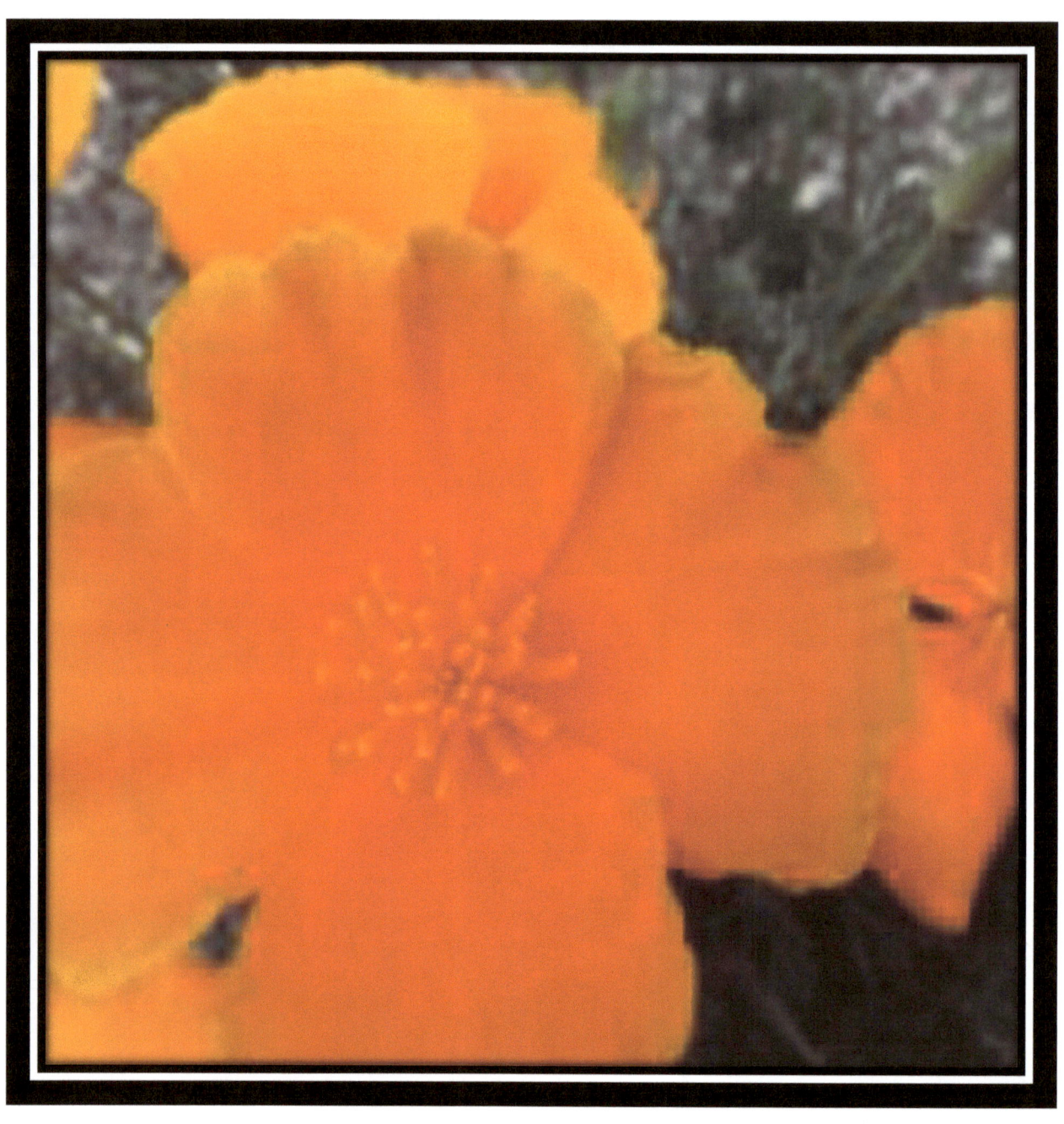

All your unfolding and molding yourself into things,

all your dramatic silences and calm pauses and chaotic coincidences... It is lovely. I love you.

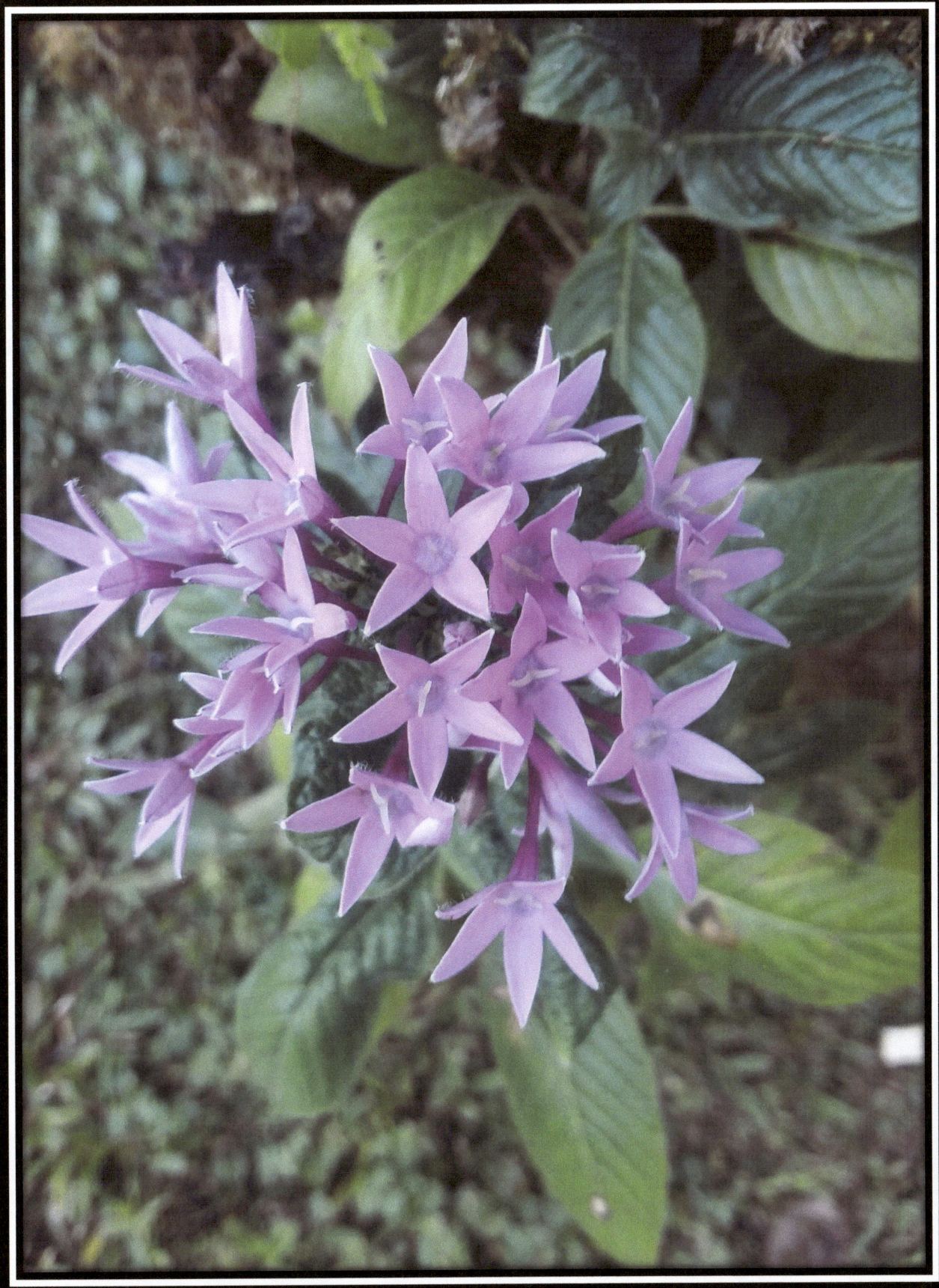

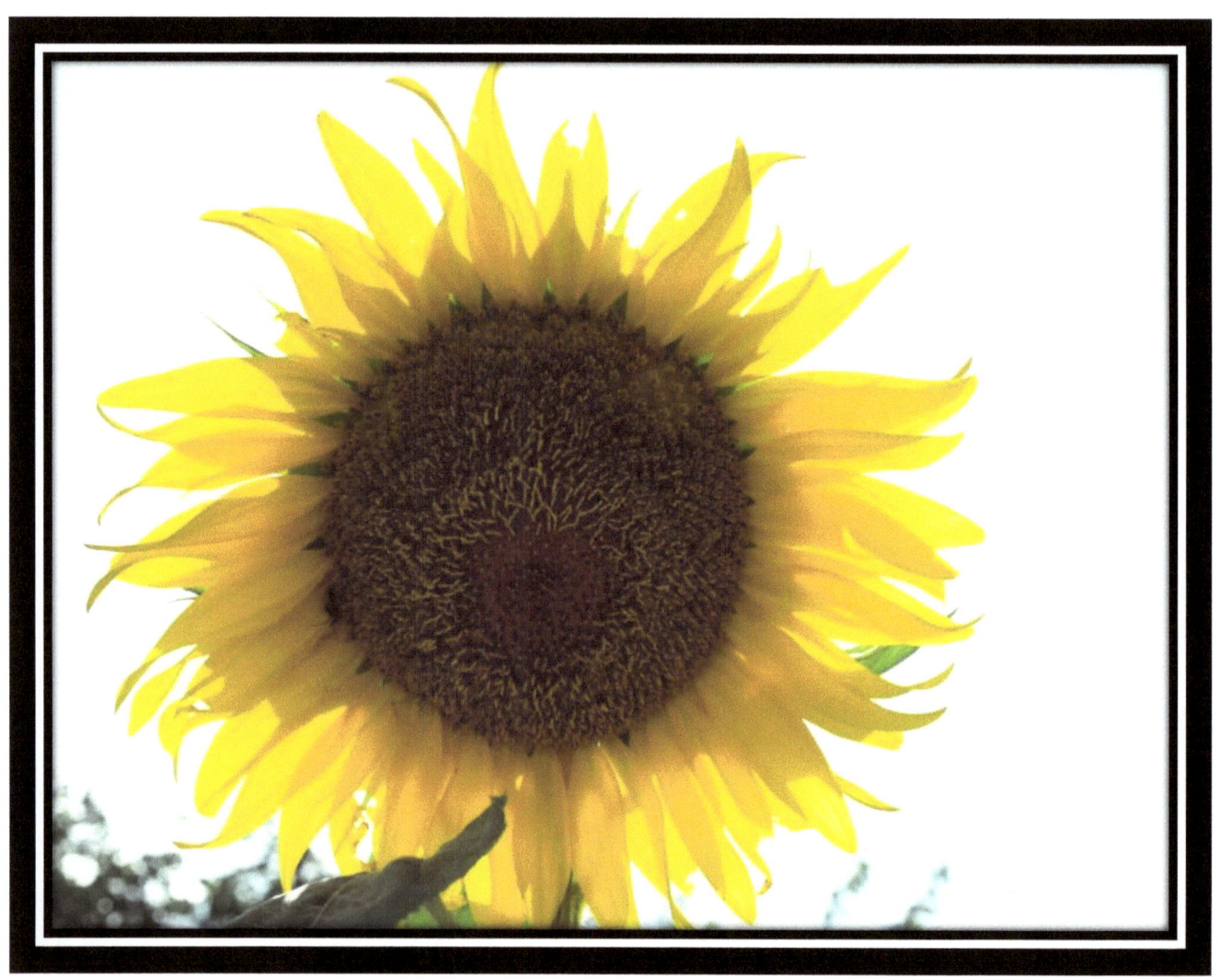

Trust. Align. Connect. Play. Let go.

I let go.

I play.

I connect.

I align.

I trust.

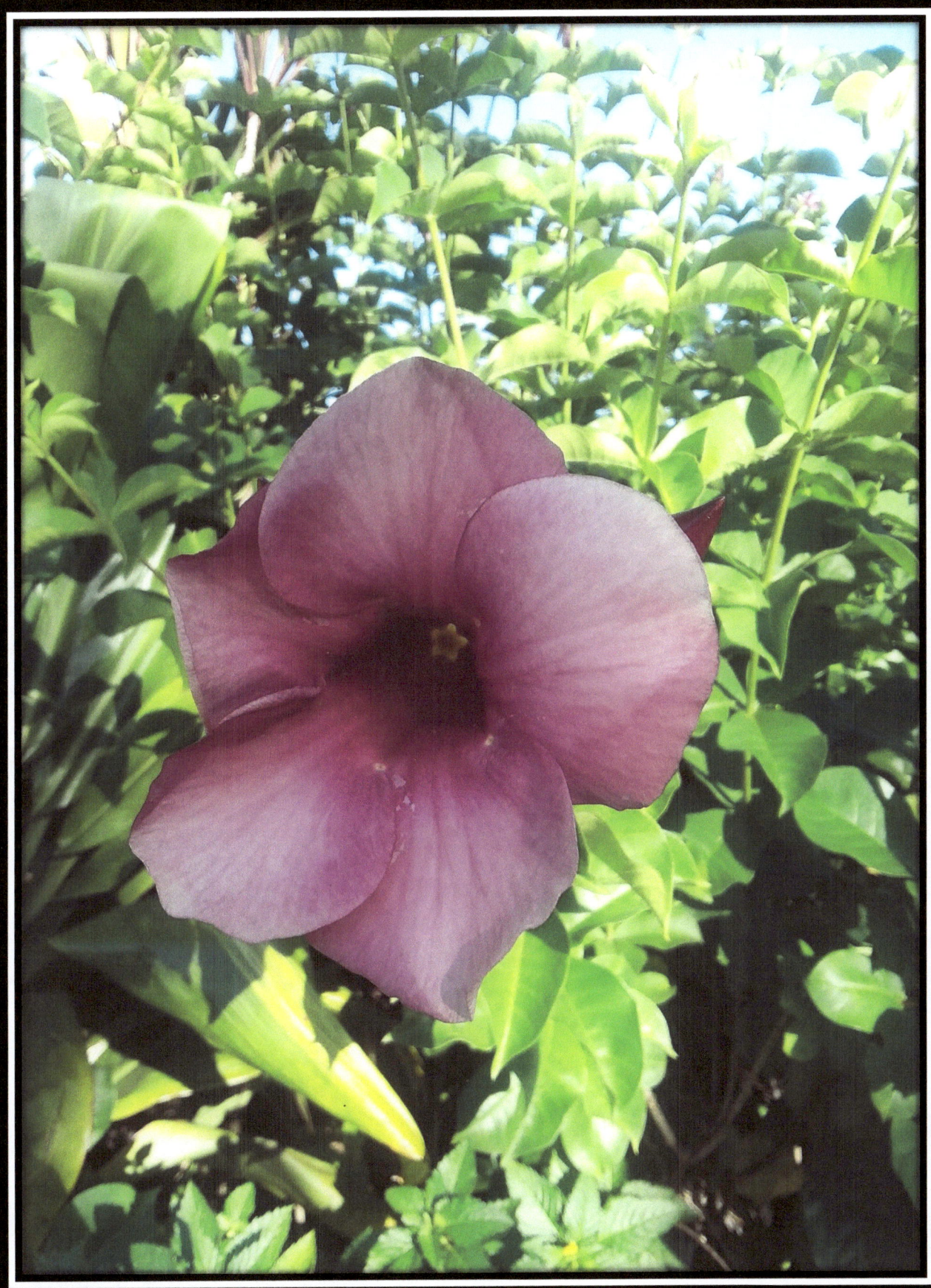

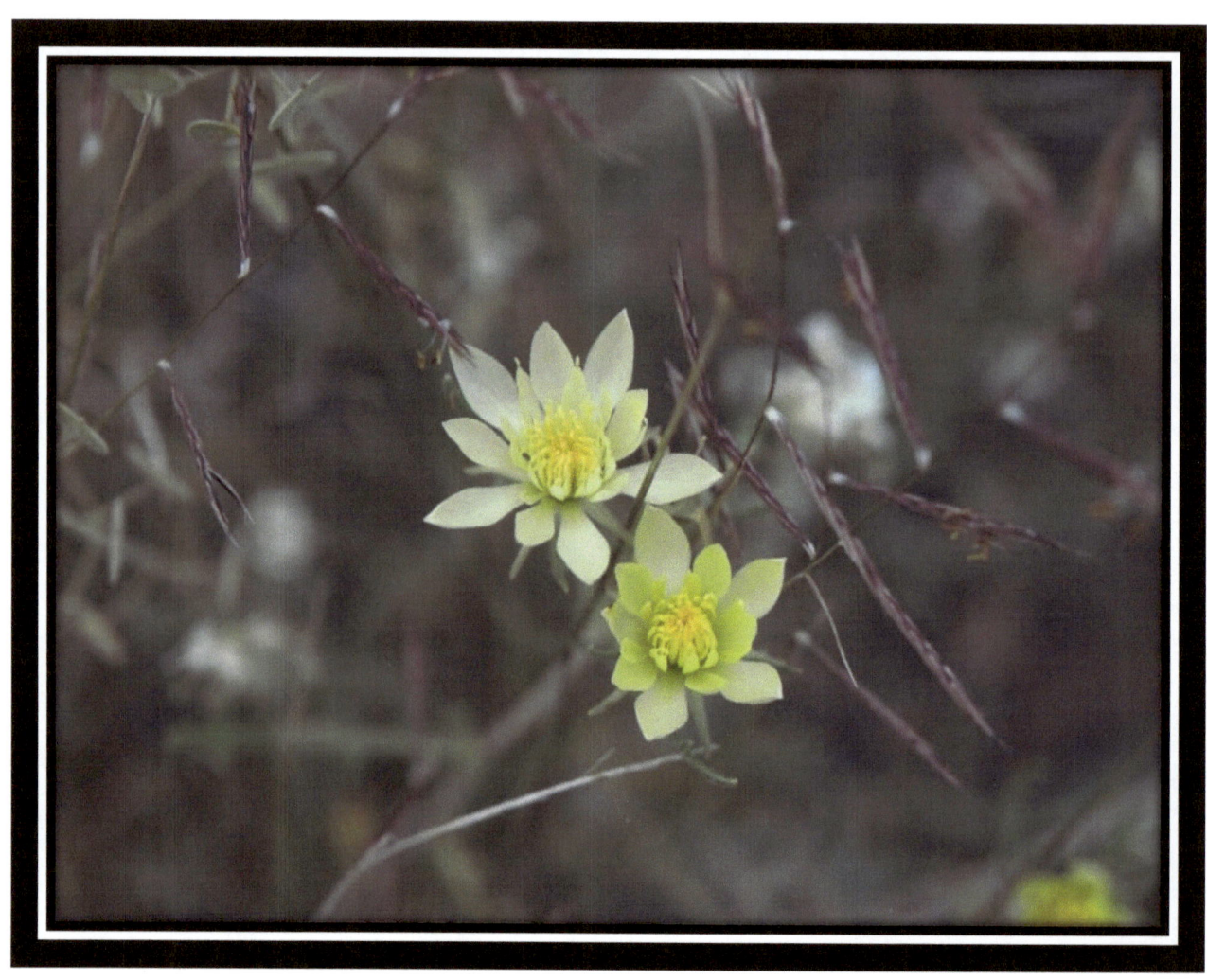

Whatever tiny shiny speck is in the middle of you,
at your core, your heart, your center,
is the same spark of warm light
that is the center of me.

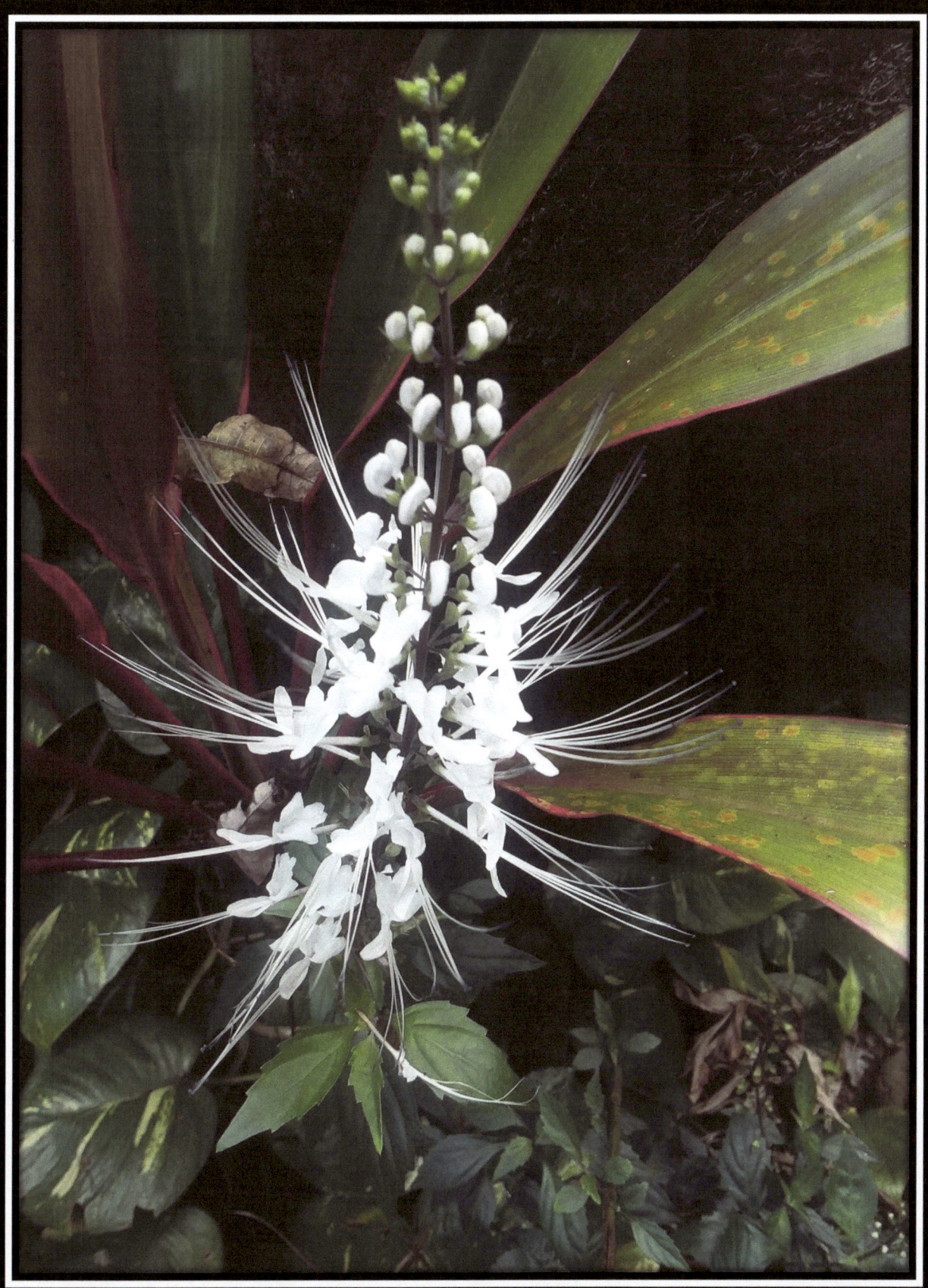

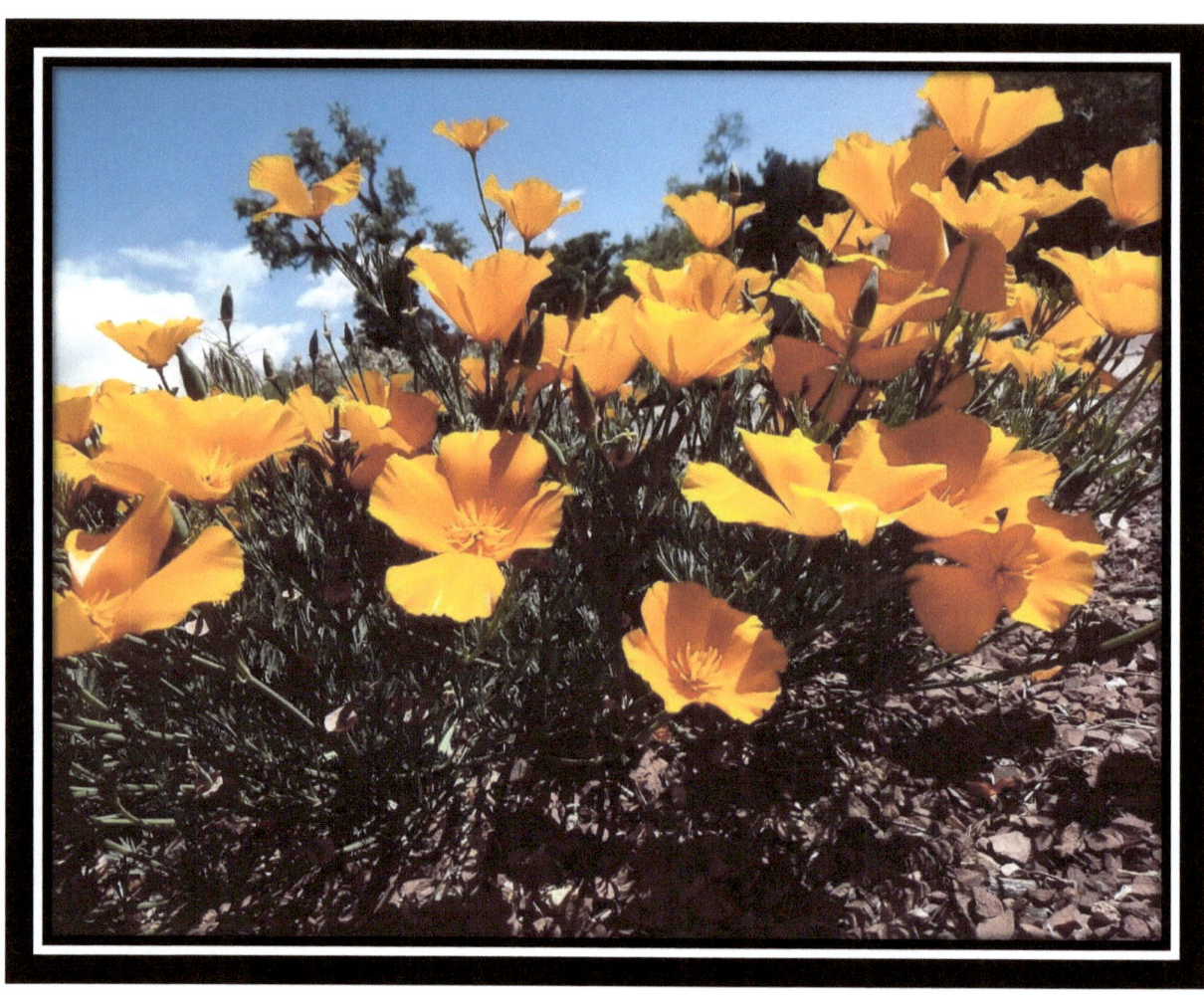

I feel whole. I feel confident. I feel complete.
I am love, loving, love.
I trust everything to unfold in perfect time.
I am aligned with my most delicious, joyful, warm,
connected, compassionate, playful self.
There is not anything missing or
incomplete or misaligned in my perception.

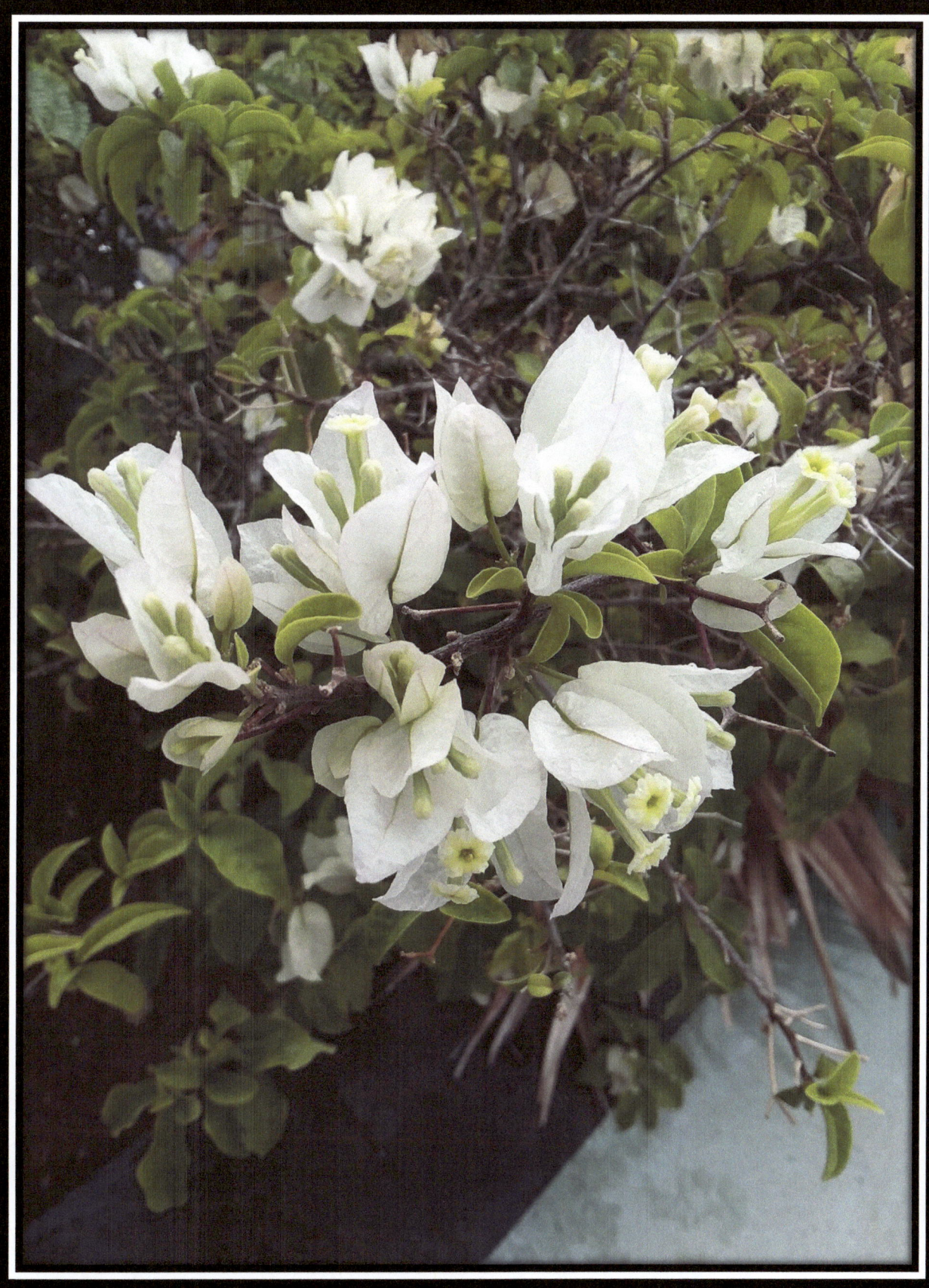

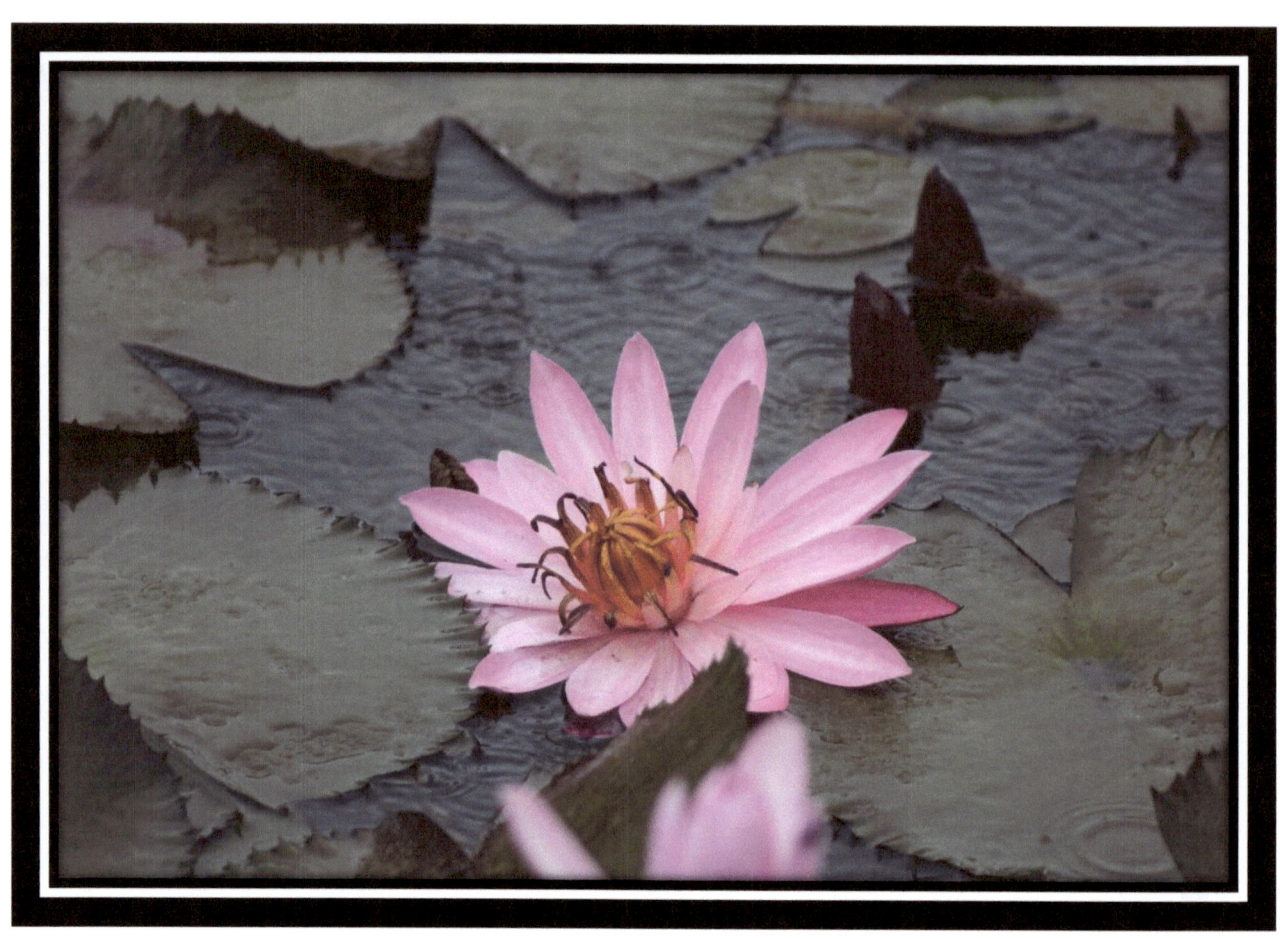

You are a natural beauty!
There is nothing I do not love
about the way you unfold in the rain.

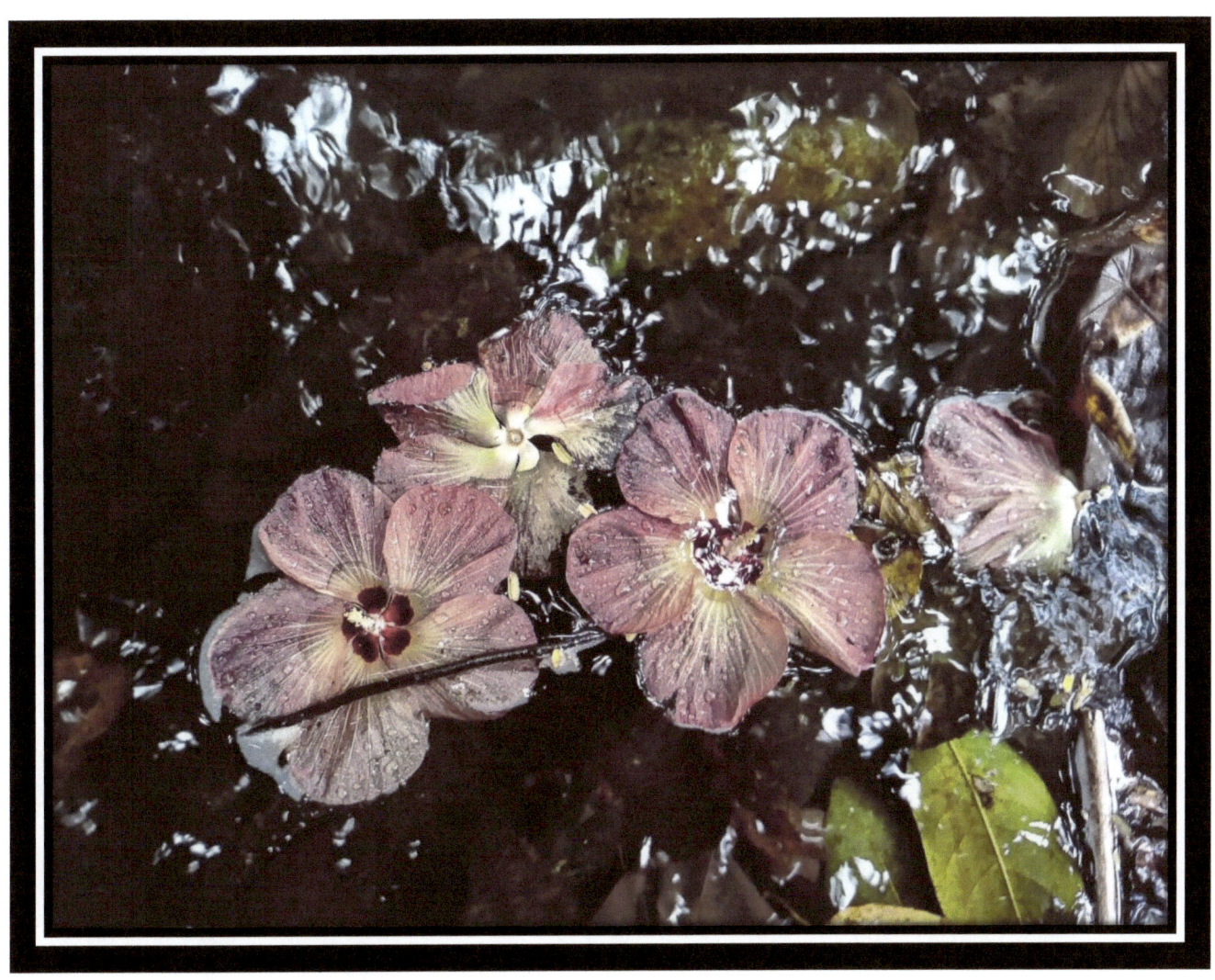

*Let's meet right where we are
and enjoy the perfection of this moment.*

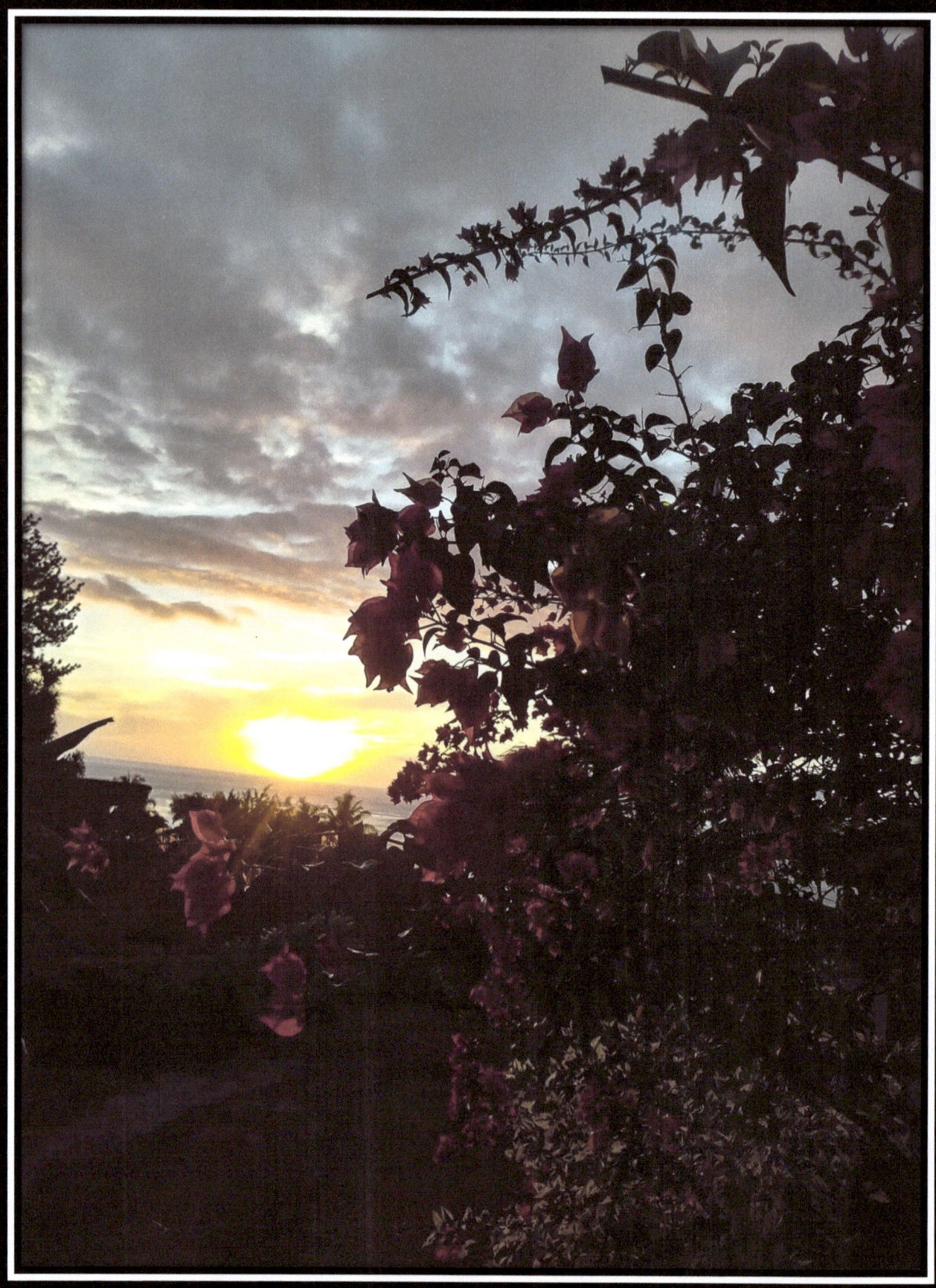

*Many thanks and much appreciation
for enjoying this book.*

*We are all one.
Be amazing and amazed.*

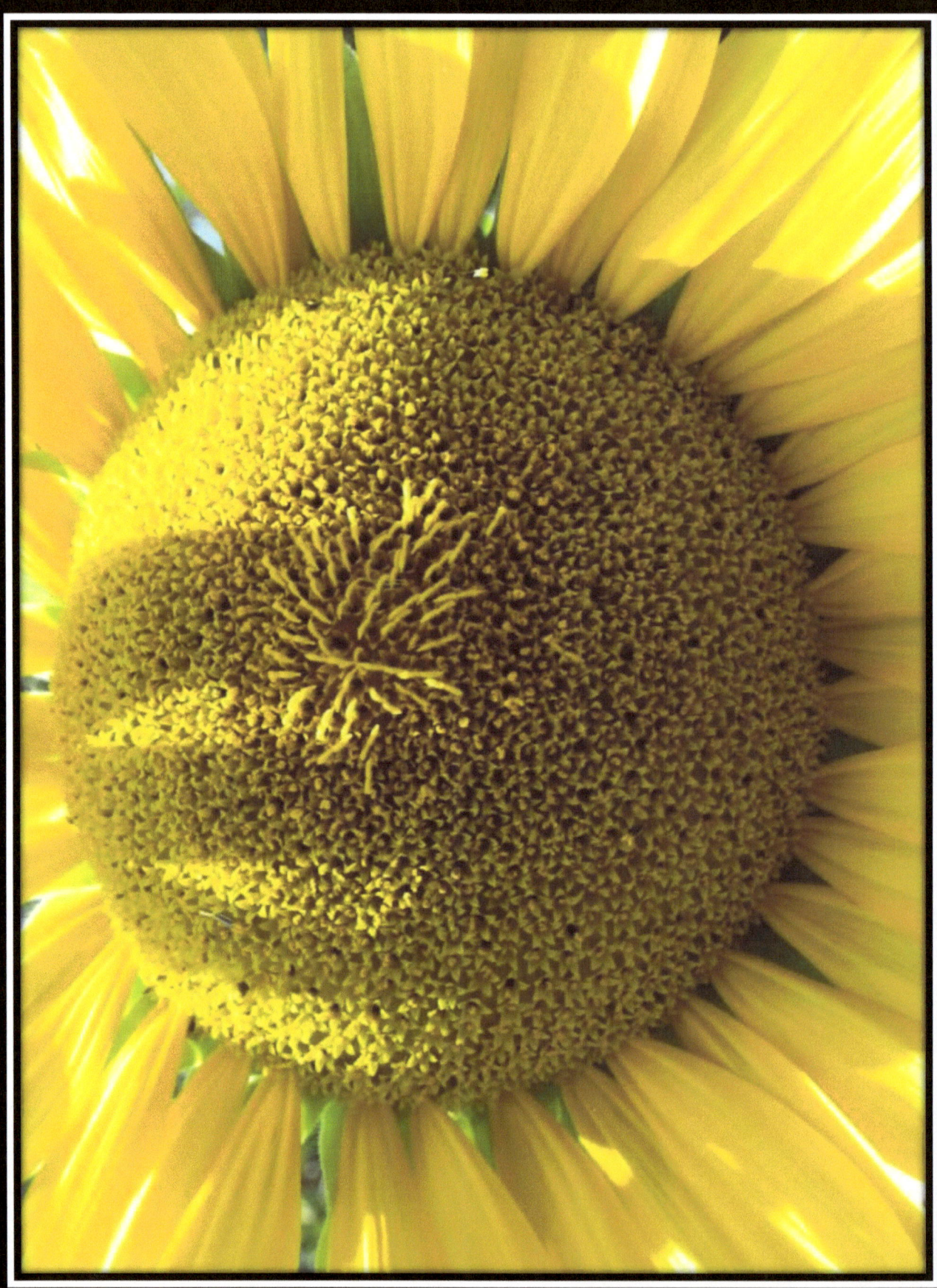

www.ingramcontent.com/pod-product-compliance
Lightning Source LLC
Chambersburg PA
CBHW051823210526
45473CB00005B/1718